From Home to School 1

Stories and Activities for Parents

Ann Gianola
Instructor, San Diego Community College District
San Diego, California

New Readers Press

From Home to School Level 1
ISBN 978-1-56420-300-7

Copyright © 2003 New Readers Press
New Readers Press
ProLiteracy's Publishing Division
104 Marcellus Street, Syracuse, New York 13204
www.newreaderspress.com

All rights reserved. No part of this book may be reproduced or transmitted in any form or by any means, electronic or mechanical, including photocopying, recording, or by any information storage and retrieval system, without permission in writing from the publisher.

Printed in the United States of America
9 8 7 6

Proceeds from the sale of New Readers Press materials support professional development, training, and technical assistance programs of ProLiteracy that benefit local literacy programs in the U.S. and around the globe.

Acquisitions Editor: Paula Schlusberg
Series Editor: Terrie Lipke
Copy Editor: Judi Lauber
Production Director: Heather Witt
Designer: Kimbrly Koennecke
Illustrations: James P. Wallace, Carolyn Boehmer
Production Specialist: Alexander Jones
Cover Design: Shelagh Clancy

Contents

Lesson 1: Don't Miss the Bus 4

Lesson 2: An Eye Exam 10

Lesson 3: A New Girl at School 16

Lesson 4: Breakfast at School 22

Lesson 5: Read More at Home 28

Lesson 6: A Classroom Volunteer 34

Lesson 7: Tests Next Week 40

Lesson 8: Sign Up for Soccer 46

Lesson 9: Fighting at School 52

Lesson 10: Too Tired for Homework 58

Lesson 11: Listen and Follow Directions 64

Lesson 12: It's Bedtime 70

Lesson 13: Expensive Shoes 76

Lesson 14: Crossing the Street 82

Lesson 15: Absent from School 88

Answer Key 94

Lesson 1

1. What time does your child get up in the morning?
2. How long does it take your child to get ready for school?

Don't Miss the Bus

Emily feels tired this morning. She doesn't want to get up. She wants to sleep. But Emily's father says, "Get up, Emily! You don't want to miss the school bus!"

"I'm up, I'm up," says Emily. She looks at the clock. It is 6:45. Her bus comes at 7:15. Emily has only 30 minutes to get ready and go to the bus stop. Emily gets dressed. Then she eats breakfast. Emily quickly brushes her teeth and combs her hair. She picks up her backpack and leaves the house.

At 7:15 Emily is running to the bus stop. She sees the yellow bus stopped at the corner. The door is closed.

The bus begins to move. "Wait!" yells Emily. "Don't leave! I'm coming!"

The bus driver stops and opens the door. "You're lucky today," says the bus driver. "I saw you coming. Don't be late again, Emily! You almost missed the bus."

Check Yes or No

Yes   No

_✓_   ___   **1.** Emily is tired this morning.

___   ___   **2.** Emily wants to get up.

___   ___   **3.** Emily's mother says, "Get up, Emily!"

___   ___   **4.** Emily looks at a watch.

___   ___   **5.** Emily's bus comes at 7:00.

___   ___   **6.** Emily has only 30 minutes to get ready.

___   ___   **7.** Emily brushes her teeth and combs her hair.

___   ___   **8.** At 7:15 Emily is walking to the bus stop.

___   ___   **9.** The yellow bus is stopped at the corner.

___   ___   **10.** The door is closed.

___   ___   **11.** The bus driver sees Emily coming.

___   ___   **12.** Emily misses the bus.

Complete the Story

| bus | corner | minutes | teeth |
| clock | driver | ✓school | tired |

John is sleeping. He doesn't want to get up for _____school_____.
                                                    1
"Get up!" says John's mother." You don't want to miss the

school _____!"
          2

John feels very _____. He wants to go back to
                      3
sleep. A few minutes later John's mother returns. John is still in

bed. "John!" she says. "Look at the _____! It's
                                              4
seven o'clock. You need to get up now. Your bus comes at

seven fifteen!"

John has only 15 _____ to get ready. He gets
                          5
dressed. He eats a piece of toast. He doesn't brush his

_____ or comb his hair.
      6

John runs to the bus stop. He sees the bus on the

_____. "Wait!" says John. But the bus
      7

_____ doesn't hear him. John misses the bus.
      8

6 Lesson 1: Don't Miss the Bus

What Happened First?

Remember the story. Then put these events in order.

____ Emily gets dressed.

____ Emily sees the yellow bus.

____ The bus driver opens the door.

____ Emily picks up her backpack and leaves the house.

_1_ Emily doesn't want to get up.

____ The bus begins to move.

____ Emily's father says, "Get up!"

Late Again

Practice the dialog with a partner.

Get up!

I'm up. I'm up.

You're not up. You're still in bed.

Now I'm up.

You need to get ready for school.

What time is it?

It's six forty-five. Your bus comes in thirty minutes.

Oh, no! I'm late again.

Lesson 1: Don't Miss the Bus

A Message from the Principal

Listen to this message on the answering machine.

> Hello, Mr. and Mrs. Mandel. This is Glen Ancheta, the principal of Foster Elementary School. I'm calling about your son, Marc. He missed the bus to school yesterday and today. We need to talk. Please call me at my office. My telephone number is 555-8794, extension 366. Thanks.

Remember the message. Then complete each sentence.

1. The principal's last name is __Ancheta__.

    Mandel   Ancheta

2. He is principal of _____ Elementary School.

    Foster   Forester

3. Mr. and Mrs. Mandel's son is named _____.

    Marc   Glen

4. The principal wants Marc's parents to call him _____.

    at home   at the office

5. The principal's telephone number is _____.

    555-9847   555-8794

8   Lesson 1: Don't Miss the Bus

Problem Solving

Your child doesn't want to get up in the morning. He or she is always late and sometimes misses the bus. Put a check next to the good ideas. Write other good ideas on the lines below.

_____ 1. I can get my child an alarm clock.

_____ 2. I can shout, "Get up!" again and again.

_____ 3. I can tell my child to go to bed earlier.

_____ 4. I can take my child to school later.

_____ 5. I can get angry with my child.

_____ 6. I can get a rooster.

_____ 7. I can reward my child for getting up on time.

✓ 8. I can _____.

✓ 9. I can _____.

Discuss with a Partner

1. Describe your child's regular morning routine.

2. Does your child take the bus to school? What other ways do children get to school?

3. Do parents need to make sure that children get up and arrive at school on time? Why or why not?

Lesson 1: Don't Miss the Bus

Lesson 2

1. Does your child have eye exams at school?
2. Does your child wear or need glasses?

An Eye Exam

The school nurse is doing eye exams this week. Layla is standing in the nurse's office. It is her turn now. The nurse is pointing to the chart. She tells Layla to cover her left eye and read the lines. The first two lines are easy to read. The letters are big. But the third line is difficult. Layla slowly reads, "E, D, F, C, Z, P." The letters are too small after the third line.

Then Layla covers her right eye. She reads two lines and stops. "Sorry," says Layla. "I can't see below the second line."

"That's OK," says the nurse. "Can you see the board in the classroom?"

"I can't see it very well," answers Layla. "And sometimes I copy things wrong. My eyes feel tired and I get a headache."

The nurse says, "Don't worry, Layla. I'm going to send a letter to your parents. They can take you to an eye doctor."

Check Yes or No

Yes   No

___ ___ **1.** The school nurse is doing ear exams.

___ ___ **2.** Layla is standing in the nurse's office.

___ ___ **3.** The nurse tells Layla to cover her left eye.

___ ___ **4.** The first two lines are difficult to read.

___ ___ **5.** The letters are big after the third line.

___ ___ **6.** Then Layla covers her right eye.

___ ___ **7.** Layla reads five lines and stops.

___ ___ **8.** Layla can't read the fourth line.

___ ___ **9.** Layla sees the board very well.

___ ___ **10.** Sometimes Layla copies things wrong.

___ ___ **11.** Layla gets headaches.

___ ___ **12.** The nurse is sending a letter to Layla's parents.

Complete the Sentences

| below | copy | headache | office |
| chart | ✓ cover | lines | parents |

1. Please ___cover___ your right eye and read.

2. Can you see _____ the third line?

3. Her eyes feel tired and she gets a _____.

4. The first two _____ are easy to read.

5. Layla is standing in the nurse's _____.

6. The nurse is pointing to the _____.

7. Sometimes I _____ things wrong.

8. The nurse is going to send a letter to Layla's _____.

Matching

Match the sentences that mean the same.

__c__ 1. I can't see it very well.   a. My head hurts.

____ 2. I copy things wrong.   b. It's time for her exam.

____ 3. I get a headache.   c. It isn't clear.

____ 4. Cover your eye.   d. I write words incorrectly.

____ 5. It is her turn now.   e. Put a hand over your eye.

12   Lesson 2: An Eye Exam

What Happened First?

Remember the story. Then put these events in order.

_____ Layla covers her right eye.

_____ Layla says that she gets headaches.

_____ Layla slowly reads, "E, D, F, C, Z, P."

_____ The nurse is going to send a letter to Layla's parents.

__1__ Layla is standing in the nurse's office.

_____ Layla covers her left eye.

_____ The nurse is pointing to the chart.

Parents Talking

Practice the dialog with a partner.

What's that?

It's a letter from the school nurse.

What does it say?

It says that our daughter had an eye exam at school. She needs to go to an eye doctor.

Do you think she needs glasses?

I don't know. Let's make an appointment for her.

Lesson 2: An Eye Exam   13

Family Eye Care

Read this ad from the yellow pages.

> ### 👁 DOCTOR ROSE LUSKIN
> **VISION CARE FOR ADULTS AND CHILDREN**
>
> Monday-Thursday 9am-6pm • Friday 9am-5pm
> 1018 Grape Street
> ## 555-6813
> Eye exams by appointment only

Remember the ad. Then complete each sentence.

1. The doctor's last name is _____.

    Larkin   Luskin

2. Vision care at this office is for _____.

    adults only   adults and children

3. Hours on Friday are _____.

    from 8:00 to 4:00   from 9:00 to 5:00

4. Dr. Luskin's address is _____.

    1180 Grape Street   1018 Grape Street

5. Dr. Luskin's telephone number is _____.

    555-6843   555-6813

Answer the Questions

1. Where does your child have eye exams?
2. Do you have eye exams?
3. When do you have eye exams?
4. Is there an eye doctor in your neighborhood?
5. What is the name of an eye doctor in your community?
6. How much does an eye exam cost?
7. Does any person in your family wear glasses?
8. How much do glasses cost?
9. Can you see better out of one eye than the other?
10. Does your child have other health exams at school?

Discuss with a Partner

1. What are doctors called who give eye exams? Who else gives eye exams?
2. Where can you take your child for an eye exam? How can you find a place that is near you?
3. Why is it important that your child see very well at school?

Lesson 3

1. Do some children feel shy on the first day of school?
2. Can everyone in your child's class speak English?

A New Girl at School

Today is Carmen's first day at a new school in the United States. Carmen is from Mexico. She is seven years old. She speaks only Spanish.

Carmen enters the class and sees many boys and girls. Everyone is speaking English. The teacher says, "We have a new student. Her name is Carmen Cruz. Welcome, Carmen!"

Everyone looks at Carmen. Carmen feels shy. The teacher tells Carmen to sit at the table next to Angela. Carmen doesn't understand the teacher. She doesn't sit down.

"*Aquí!*" says Angela. That means *here* in Spanish. Carmen walks over to the empty chair next to Angela. She sits down. Angela speaks Spanish too. She turns to Carmen and says, "Don't worry, I came from Mexico last year. English is easy."

Carmen smiles. She feels better. She can learn English like the other boys and girls. And she has a new friend.

Check Yes or No

Yes   No

___ ___   1. It is Carmen's first day at a new school.

___ ___   2. Carmen is from Puerto Rico.

___ ___   3. Carmen is eight years old.

___ ___   4. Carmen speaks Spanish and English.

___ ___   5. Everyone in the class is speaking English.

___ ___   6. Carmen feels tired.

___ ___   7. The teacher tells Carmen to sit next to Angela.

___ ___   8. Carmen understands the teacher.

___ ___   9. *Aquí* means *there* in Spanish.

___ ___ 10. Carmen sits next to Angela.

___ ___ 11. Angela came from Mexico last year.

___ ___ 12. Carmen has a new friend.

Complete the Story

| chair | friends | only | Welcome |
| empty | Japanese | shy | years |

Today is Akio's first day at a new school in the United States. Akio is from Japan. He is nine _____ old.
                                                                    1
He speaks _____ Japanese.
            2

Akio enters the class. Everyone is speaking English. The teacher says, "We have a new student. His name is Akio Ito. _____, Akio!"
                                                                    3

Everyone looks at Akio. He feels _____. The
                                    4
teacher tells Akio to sit next to Jason. Akio doesn't understand.

Jason stands up. He says, "Here!" He points to the _____ chair at his table. Now Akio understands.
       5
He walks over to the _____ and sits down.
                        6

Jason smiles at Akio. Jason doesn't speak _____,
                                              7
and Akio doesn't speak English. But they can be _____.
                                                    8

18   Lesson 3: A New Girl at School

Check the Feelings

Put a check next to the feelings a child might have on the first day of school. Write other emotions below.

___ excited   ___ nervous   ___ thrilled

___ lonely   ___ cheerful   ___ scared

___ sad   ___ confused   ___ proud

_____   _____   _____

Meeting the Teacher

Practice the dialog with a partner.

Hello. My name is Maria Cruz. My daughter Carmen is a new student. She is in your class.

It's very nice to meet you, Mrs. Cruz.

Carmen doesn't speak any English. Is that a problem?

No, it's not. We can help her.

She is also very nervous.

Don't worry. Your daughter is going to be fine.

Lesson 3: A New Girl at School

Personal Information Form

Fill out Carmen's form.

ABC ELEMENTARY SCHOOL

Last Name _____

First Name _____

Age ____

Native Country _____

Native Language _____

Make a List

List things for Carmen to bring to school on the first day.

1. _backpack_　　4. _____

2. _____　　5. _____

3. _____　　6. _____

List things that children should not bring to school.

1. _toys_　　4. _____

2. _____　　5. _____

3. _____　　6. _____

Lesson 3: A New Girl at School

Problem Solving

Your child doesn't want to go to a new school. He or she feels nervous and scared. Put a check next to the good ideas. Write other ideas on the lines below.

___ 1. I can visit the school with my child.

___ 2. I can introduce my child to the teacher.

___ 3. I can ignore my child's feelings.

___ 4. I can tell my child that he or she is acting like a baby.

___ 5. I can wait until my child wants to go to school.

___ 6. I can ask the teacher to find a friend for my child.

✔ 7. I can _____.

✔ 8. I can _____.

Discuss with a Partner

1. Tell how you felt on your first day at a new school.

2. Is it easy for children to learn a new language? How long will it take for Carmen to learn English? How long does it take for an adult to learn a new language?

3. Are there any children from other countries in your child's class? Where are they from? What languages do they speak?

Lesson 4

1. What does your child usually eat for breakfast?
2. Is there a breakfast program at your child's school?

Breakfast at School

It's early in the morning, and Lamar is getting ready for school. He needs to leave the house early to catch the bus at 6:45. His father is in the kitchen. "Lamar," says his father. "Do you have time for a bowl of cereal or a piece of toast?"

"No," answers Lamar. "It's late. I don't have time. I'm going to eat at school."

Lamar's father is happy that there is a breakfast program at school. He doesn't want his son to be hungry. He knows that a good breakfast helps Lamar stay healthy. It also helps him pay attention in school and be a good student.

Lamar rides the bus for 45 minutes and arrives at school at 7:30. Then Lamar feels very hungry. He goes to the school cafeteria. They serve breakfast every day. Today there are pancakes and orange juice. Lamar has 10 minutes to eat.

The bell rings at 7:40. Lamar throws away his empty juice container. He picks up his backpack. It's time to go to class.

Check Yes or No

Yes   No

___ ___ 1. Lamar is getting ready for school.

___ ___ 2. Lamar catches the bus at 7:00.

___ ___ 3. Lamar's mother is in the kitchen.

___ ___ 4. Lamar has time to eat a bowl of cereal.

___ ___ 5. There is a breakfast program at school.

___ ___ 6. Lamar's father wants his son to eat.

___ ___ 7. A good breakfast helps Lamar stay healthy.

___ ___ 8. Lamar feels very hungry.

___ ___ 9. Lamar goes to the school office.

___ ___ 10. Today there are pancakes and milk.

___ ___ 11. The bell rings at 7:40.

Lesson 4: Breakfast at School

Underline the Word from the Story

1. It's early in the (<u>morning</u>/afternoon).
2. His father is in the (bedroom/kitchen).
3. Lamar's father doesn't want his son to be (hungry/angry).
4. A good breakfast helps Lamar be a good (father/student).
5. Lamar goes to the school (auditorium/cafeteria).
6. The school serves breakfast (every Monday/every day).

Unscramble the Sentences

Write the sentence on the line.

1. ready   Lamar   is   school.   for   getting

   <u>Lamar is getting ready for school.</u>

2. time   Do   of   cereal?   for   a   have   bowl   you

   _____

3. school.   is   at   There   program   a   breakfast

   _____

4. good   pay   A   attention.   breakfast   helps   him

   _____

Lesson 4: Breakfast at School

Check the Breakfast Foods

Put a check next to the food and drinks that your child has for breakfast. Write other breakfast foods below.

___ cereal ___ milk ___ banana

___ pancakes ___ orange juice ___ waffles

___ eggs ___ muffin ___ bacon

___ toast ___ sausage ___ fruit

_____ _____ _____ _____

What's for Breakfast?

Practice the dialog with a partner.

Do you have time to eat something?

No, thanks. I'm going to eat at school.

What are they having today?

I'm not sure. It's on the menu.

The menu says cereal and milk on Tuesday. Is that OK?

Yes. I like that.

This Week's Breakfast Menu

Read the school breakfast menu.

School Breakfast

Monday	orange juice, cereal, graham crackers, milk
Tuesday	applesauce, breakfast cheese pizza, milk
Wednesday	berry juice, French toast, syrup, milk
Thursday	chilled peaches, bagel with margarine, milk
Friday	orange juice, fruit yogurt, banana bread, milk

Remember the menu. Then complete each sentence.

1. Your son can eat breakfast cheese pizza on _____.

   Tuesday   Wednesday

2. Your daughter can drink orange juice on _____.

   Monday and Friday   Thursday and Friday

3. There is no juice on _____.

   Tuesday or Wednesday   Tuesday or Thursday

4. There is milk _____.

   on Monday and Thursday   every day

5. On Thursday the fruit is _____.

   berries   peaches

Lesson 4: Breakfast at School

Answer the Questions

1. Does your child always eat breakfast?
2. Does your child's school have a breakfast program?
3. What does your child like to eat for breakfast?
4. What time does your child leave the house?
5. How long does it take your child to get to school?
6. Does your child's school have a cafeteria?
7. Does the cafeteria serve breakfast and lunch?
8. Does your child usually bring a lunch to school?

Discuss with a Partner

1. Do you think it's important for adults and children to have a good breakfast? Why or why not?
2. Your child is late for school. He or she doesn't have time to eat breakfast at home. There is no breakfast program at school. What can you do?
3. What does your family eat for breakfast on weekdays? Do you eat a bigger breakfast on the weekends? What do you eat? What is the biggest meal of the day for your family?

Lesson 5

1. Do you go to parent and teacher conferences?
2. Does your child read a lot at home?

Read More at Home

It is 4:30 P.M. Pedro's mother and father are sitting at a table in his classroom. They are talking to Pedro's third-grade teacher, Miss Soto. It is a parent and teacher conference. Miss Soto says, "Pedro is a very nice boy. I am happy that your son is in my class."

Pedro's parents smile. They feel proud of their son. "Thank you," Pedro's mother says.

"But I am concerned about Pedro's reading," says Miss Soto. "It's difficult for him. He is behind the other students. He needs to read more at home."

"I understand," says Pedro's father. "But he doesn't

want to read at home. I am worried about that too. He wants to play baseball."

Miss Soto explains that reading is very important. She says that good students are also good readers. She tells Pedro's parents to take him to the library. He can check out books about baseball. "Pedro is very smart," says Miss Soto. "You can help him be a strong student."

Check Yes or No

Yes No

___ ___ 1. It is 4:00 P.M.

___ ___ 2. Pedro's mother and father are at home.

___ ___ 3. Pedro's parents are talking to Miss Soto.

___ ___ 4. Pedro is a very nice boy.

___ ___ 5. Pedro's parents are angry with their son.

___ ___ 6. Miss Soto is concerned about Pedro's reading.

___ ___ 7. Pedro is ahead of the other students.

___ ___ 8. Pedro reads a lot at home.

___ ___ 9. Pedro wants to play baseball.

___ ___ 10. Pedro needs to go to the library.

___ ___ 11. Pedro is very smart.

Lesson 5: Read More at Home   29

What Is the Category?

arithmetic	✓librarian	reading	teacher
concerned	parent	spelling	worried
happy	proud	student	writing

People   **Emotions**   **School Subjects**

1. _librarian_   1. _____   1. _____

2. _____   2. _____   2. _____

3. _____   3. _____   3. _____

4. _____   4. _____   4. _____

Same Meaning

Copy the word or phrase from the story that has the same meaning as the phrase below.

1. very intelligent _very smart_____

2. make a happy facial expression _____

3. It isn't easy for him. _____

4. not reading as well as other children _____

5. meeting for parents and the teacher _____

Check the Books

Put a check next to the kinds of books that interest your child. Write other kinds of books below.

___ books about sports   ___ comic books

___ books about nature   ___ adventure stories

___ mysteries   ___ books about science

___ fiction   ___ fairy tales

___ books about animals   ___ biographies

___ history books   ___ picture books

_____   _____

Checking Out Books

Practice the dialog with a partner.

How do I get a library card?

It's easy. You just need some identification.

Can I check out books today?

Sure. Here is your card.

When are the books due?

You need to return them in three weeks.

Library Information

Listen to the library's telephone recording.

> You have reached the Mission Park branch of the public library. The library is located at 5148 Sierra Street between 11th and 12th Avenues. Our hours are Monday and Wednesday, noon to 8:00 P.M.; Tuesday, Thursday, Friday, and Saturday, from 9:30 A.M. to 5:30 P.M. We are open on Sunday from 1:00 to 5:00 P.M. We are closed on holidays.

Remember the message. Then complete each sentence.

1. This is the _____ branch of the public library.

    Mission Park   Sierra

2. It is between _____ Avenues.

    10th and 11th   11th and 12th

3. The hours are _____, noon to 8:00 P.M.

    Monday and Thursday   Monday and Wednesday

4. It is open on Friday and Saturday _____.

    from 9:30 A.M. to 5:30 P.M.   from noon to 8:00 P.M.

5. The library is _____ on Sundays.

    open   closed

32 Lesson 5: Read More at Home

Answer the Questions

1. How many times a year do you go to parent and teacher conferences?
2. What is the name of your child's teacher?
3. Is your child reading a lot?
4. Is reading difficult for your child?
5. Does your child need to read more at home?
6. What does your child like to do at home?
7. Is there a library in your neighborhood?
8. Where is the nearest public library?
9. What are the days and times the public library is open?
10. Do you have a library card?

Discuss with a Partner

1. What things are parents and teachers concerned about?
2. What is the difference between a school library and a public library? Where do you prefer to borrow books? Why?
3. Tell about one of your favorite books for children.

Lesson 6

1. Do you volunteer in your child's classroom?
2. What kind of things do classroom volunteers do?

A Classroom Volunteer

Lili is in the first grade. Every Tuesday her mother, Mei Yong, volunteers in the classroom. Mei helps in Lili's classroom between 9:00 and 11:00 A.M.

Sometimes Mei helps the children one at a time.

Mei helps David when he raises his hand. She helps Eve when Eve doesn't understand a math problem.

Mei also works with small groups of children. She helps them learn addition. She holds up flash cards. "What is 3 + 4?" she asks. "What is 5 + 2?" The children like Mrs. Yong.

The teacher is happy to have Mei in the class. Mei does many things to help her. She corrects papers for the teacher. Mei also hands out school announcements for the children to take home.

Lili is very happy her mother comes to class on Tuesday. She feels proud. Mei wants to spend time in Lili's class too. She sees that Lili is doing well in school. Mei likes to volunteer.

Check Yes or No

Yes   No

___   ___   **1.** Lili is in the fifth grade.

___   ___   **2.** Mei Yong volunteers every Tuesday.

___   ___   **3.** Mei helps in the class between 9:00 and 1:00.

___   ___   **4.** Mei helps David when he raises his hand.

___   ___   **5.** Mei helps Eve correct papers.

___   ___   **6.** Mei works with large groups of children.

___   ___   **7.** Mei helps the children learn Chinese.

___   ___   **8.** The children like Mrs. Yong.

___   ___   **9.** The teacher is happy to have Mei volunteer.

___   ___   **10.** Lili is sad when her mother comes to class.

___   ___   **11.** Mei wants to spend time in Lili's class.

Underline the Word from the Story

1. Lili is in the first (class/grade).

2. Mei volunteers every (Tuesday/Thursday).

3. Mei helps in the (office/classroom).

4. Mei volunteers (before/between) 9:00 and 11:00 A.M.

5. Mei helps David when he raises his (hand/voice).

6. Mei helps the children learn (subtraction/addition).

7. The (teachers/students) like Mrs. Yong.

Unscramble the Sentences

Write the sentence on the line.

1. the   grade.   is   in   Lili   first

   _____

2. classroom.   Her   the   volunteers   in   mother

   _____

3. helps   She   addition.   them   learn

   _____

4. the   papers   Mei   for   corrects   teacher.

   _____

Lesson 6: A Classroom Volunteer

Who Says That?

Mei or Lili

1. "I'm here to volunteer." _____

2. "That's my Mom!" _____

3. "I am Mei Yong's daughter." _____

4. "What is 3 + 4?" _____

5. "I am in first grade." _____

Helping in Class

Practice the dialog with a partner.

How can I help today?

Will you do math flash cards in small groups?

Sure. Is there anything else?

You can walk around and help students with the work sheet.

Do you have anything for me to correct?

You can correct the spelling papers on my desk if you have time.

Who Needs Help?

Circle the picture of each child who needs help.
What is each child doing?

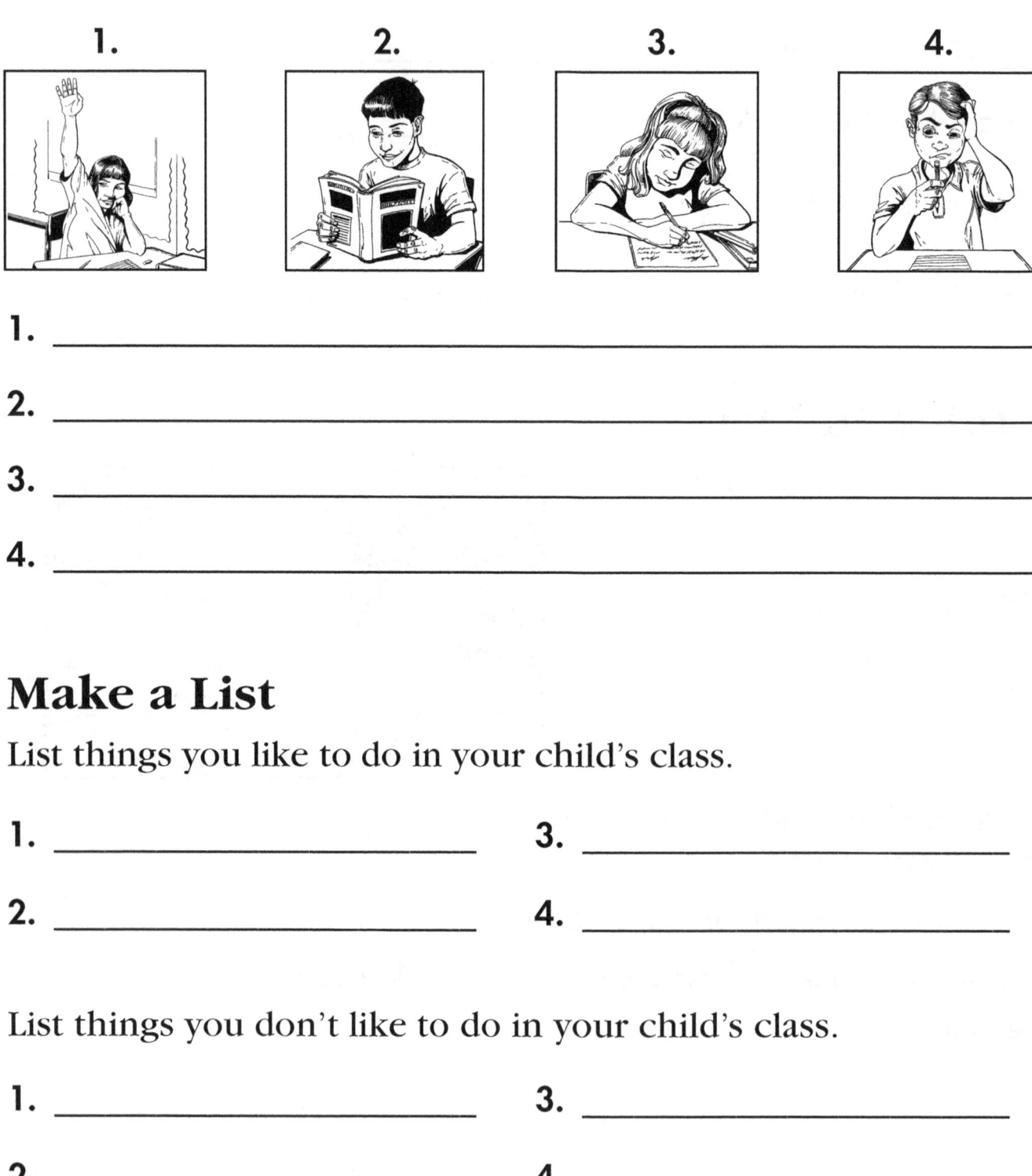

1. _____
2. _____
3. _____
4. _____

Make a List

List things you like to do in your child's class.

1. _____   3. _____

2. _____   4. _____

List things you don't like to do in your child's class.

1. _____   3. _____

2. _____   4. _____

Problem Solving

The teacher asks you to correct some spelling tests. You're not sure how to spell all of the words correctly. Put a check next to the good ideas. Write other good ideas on the lines below.

____ 1. I can ask the teacher for a list of the correct words.

____ 2. I can guess how the words are spelled.

____ 3. I can look up the words in the dictionary.

____ 4. I can ask one of the students to help me.

____ 5. I can say that I forgot my glasses.

____ 6. I can ignore the teacher and do something else.

____ 7. I can explain that spelling is difficult for me.

✓ 8. I can _____.

✓ 9. I can _____.

Discuss with a Partner

1. Is it important for parents to volunteer in the classroom? Why or why not?

2. Why is it difficult for some parents to volunteer in class? How can parents support the school in other ways?

Lesson 7

1. Does your child have testing at school?
2. How can you help your child prepare for a test?

Tests Next Week

Juan opens his backpack and takes out a piece of paper. He gives it to his mother. It's a note from Juan's fourth-grade teacher. Juan's mother reads the note. It says that all students need to take tests at school next week.

The tests will be Monday through Friday from 9:00 to 11:00. There are tests in reading, math, language, science, and other subjects. They check what the children understand in these areas.

The teacher wants the students to do well on the tests. She suggests that the children go to bed early. She also says that a good breakfast is very important. Tired and hungry children do not take tests very well. The teacher also wants the students to arrive at school on time.

Next week Juan's mother makes sure he goes to bed early. She gives him a good breakfast every morning. Juan arrives at school on time. Juan is ready for testing.

Check Yes or No

Yes   No

____ ____ **1.** Juan opens his notebook.

____ ____ **2.** Juan gives his mother a piece of paper.

____ ____ **3.** The paper is a note from Juan's school principal.

____ ____ **4.** Students need to take tests next month.

____ ____ **5.** The tests will be Monday through Friday.

____ ____ **6.** The tests will be from 9:00 to 11:00.

____ ____ **7.** The tests check physical education.

____ ____ **8.** The teacher recommends going to bed late.

____ ____ **9.** A good breakfast is very important.

____ ____ **10.** Tired and hungry children take tests well.

____ ____ **11.** Juan arrives at school late next week.

____ ____ **12.** Juan is ready for testing.

Lesson 7: Tests Next Week **41**

Complete the Sentences

| backpack | language | ready | tests |
| important | note | suggests | tired |

1. The teacher _____ that you go to bed early.

2. Are you _____ for testing?

3. This test will check what you understand in _____.

4. Hungry and _____ children do not take tests well.

5. I have a piece of paper in my _____.

6. Is that a _____ from your teacher?

7. A good breakfast is very _____.

8. All students need to take _____ next week.

Matching

Match the parts of the sentences.

____ 1. Make sure   a. what a child understands.

____ 2. The teacher wants b. ready for testing.

____ 3. The tests check   c. him a good breakfast.

____ 4. My child is   d. he goes to bed early.

____ 5. The tests will be e. the students to do well.

____ 6. His mother gives   f. Monday through Friday.

Check the Papers

Put a check next to the papers your child brings home from school. Write other kinds of papers below.

____ information forms

____ school newsletter

____ report card

____ permission slips

____ homework

____ activities announcements

____ health news

____ school holiday notices

____ progress reports

____ fund-raising material

____ volunteer requests

____ warnings

_____

_____

Rest before the Test

Practice the dialog with a partner.

Are you almost ready for bed?

No, I never go to bed this early.

Sorry, but you need to go to bed early for the next few days.

Why?

You have tests at school all week. I want you to get a lot of rest and do well.

Oh, that's right. I forgot.

Lesson 7: Tests Next Week

A Letter to Parents

Read the letter from school.

Dear Parents,
During the week of May 1, all students except kindergartners will be taking a series of achievement tests. These tests check your child's basic skills in reading, mathematics, language arts, science, and social studies. A nutritious breakfast and an early bedtime are very important. We would also appreciate all students arriving at school on time.

Remember the letter. Then complete each sentence.

1. This letter is for the _____.

    parents   students

2. Testing begins the week of _____.

    May 1   March 1

3. Kindergartners _____ taking the tests.

    will not be   will be

4. The tests check basic _____ in many areas.

    schools   skills

5. A _____ breakfast is very important.

    nutritious   light

Answer the Questions

1. Does your child take achievement tests at school?
2. What are the names of the tests?
3. What do the tests check?
4. What time of year do students take these tests?
5. Do you receive a letter about testing?
6. Do you see the results of your child's tests?
7. Do you understand the results?
8. Do you prepare a good breakfast before testing?
9. Does your child go to bed early before testing?
10. Do you make sure that your child arrives at school on time?

Discuss with a Partner

1. Do you think testing in school is important? Why or why not?
2. Do you think tests are effective in checking what your child understands? Why or why not?
3. In what ways can you help your child during testing time?

Lesson 8

1. What sports can children participate in?
2. What sports or activities does your community offer?

Sign Up for Soccer

Alfonso picks up his daughter Marla every day after school. Today Marla gets in the car. She is very excited. "Can I sign up for soccer at the youth center?" asks Marla. "Oh, please say yes!"

Alfonso knows that soccer is the same as football in Mexico. Sometimes he sees boys and girls playing soccer at a field near his house. The children wear uniforms and run around. Soccer is very good exercise. The children look happy. "I really want to play," says Marla. "My friends Kim and Margarita are playing soccer. I want to play too!"

Alfonso needs more information. He doesn't know the day and time of practice. He doesn't know where they play games. He doesn't know how much money it costs to play soccer.

Tonight Alfonso can call Kim's parents and ask questions. He can't say yes or no right now. Alfonso says, "We'll see, Marla. We'll see."

Check Yes or No

Yes   No

___ ___   1. Alfonso picks up his daughter every day.

___ ___   2. His daughter's name is Marta.

___ ___   3. Marla wants to sign up for soccer.

___ ___   4. Soccer is the same as baseball in Mexico.

___ ___   5. Only boys play soccer.

___ ___   6. Children play soccer near Alfonso's house.

___ ___   7. The children wear uniforms and run around.

___ ___   8. Alfonso needs more information.

___ ___   9. Alfonso doesn't know where they play games.

___ ___   10. Alfonso knows that soccer is very expensive.

___ ___   11. Alfonso plans to call Margarita's parents.

Complete the Story

excited	girls	money	sign up
friends	information	questions	uniforms

Leslie picks up her sons Patrick and Daniel every day after school. Today Patrick and Daniel are very _____.
1

The boys ask, "Can we _____ for basketball?"
2

Leslie sees boys and _____ playing basketball
3
at the city recreation center near her apartment. The children wear _____ and run around. They look happy.
4
"We really want to play," says Patrick.

"All of our _____ are playing," says Daniel.
5

Leslie needs more _____. She doesn't know the
6
day and time of practice. She doesn't know how much _____ it costs to play basketball. Tonight Leslie can
7
call the recreation center and ask _____. She can't
8
say yes or no right now. Leslie says, "We'll see, boys."

48   Lesson 8: Sign Up for Soccer

Check the Sports

Put a check next to the sports children can play in your neighborhood. Write the names of other sports below.

___ soccer	___ softball	___ football
___ basketball	___ running	___ swimming
___ baseball	___ karate	___ lacrosse
___ tennis	___ hockey	___ gymnastics
_____	_____	_____

Calling a Parent for Information

Practice the dialog with a partner.

Do you know what day soccer practice is?

Yes, they practice every Wednesday.

And what time?

Practice begins at four o'clock and ends at five thirty.

Oh, that's a problem. I don't get off work until five o'clock.

Maybe I can take the kids at four o'clock and you can pick them up at five thirty.

That's a great idea.

Lesson 8: Sign Up for Soccer 49

Youth Soccer Information

Listen to the recreation center phone recording.

This is the Mountain View Youth Center. We are located at 1251 Ivy Street. Soccer signups are Saturday, May 21, from 9:00 to 12:00. The cost for soccer is $75. This includes the price of the uniform. Also, please bring a copy of your child's birth certificate. Thank you.

Remember the message. Then complete each sentence.

1. The youth center is located at _____ Street.

    1251 Ivy   1251 Ives

2. Soccer signups are on _____, May 21.

    Sunday   Saturday

3. The signups are _____.

    from 9:00 to 12:00   from 8:00 to 12:00

4. The cost includes the price of the _____.

    unit   uniform

5. Parents need to bring a copy of their child's
    _____.

    birth date   birth certificate

Lesson 8: Sign Up for Soccer

Problem Solving

Your child wants to play a sport. You're not sure that you have the time for practices and games. Put a check next to the good ideas. Write other good ideas on the lines below.

_____ 1. I can ask other parents for help.

_____ 2. I can explain to my child that I don't have time.

_____ 3. I can tell my child that he or she is too young.

_____ 4. I can change my work schedule.

_____ 5. I can tell my child that sports are dangerous.

_____ 6. I can check the schedule for other sports.

_____ 7. I can talk to the coach.

✔ 8. I can _____.

✔ 9. I can _____.

Discuss with a Partner

1. What is a sport that your child plays or a sport that you played when you were young? How do you play it?

2. Do you think it's important for children to do what their friends are doing? Why or why not?

3. When you can't answer yes or no to your child, what do you say?

Lesson 8: Sign Up for Soccer

Lesson 9

1. What rules are there at your child's school?
2. Do you report problems your child has at school?

Fighting at School

Max comes home from school at 4:00. His face is dirty. His shirt is torn. Max is very sad. Max's mother sees him and asks, "What's wrong?"

Max doesn't answer. Then he begins to cry. He tells his mother that he feels afraid. He says that he doesn't want to go to school anymore.

Max's mother is surprised. She asks Max why he is upset. Max tells his mother about a big boy at school. The boy's name is Fred. Fred is mean. He hits and kicks people. He always wants to fight. "Look at my shirt," says Max. "Fred did this!"

Max's mother gives him a hug. She tells Max that fighting is bad. Then she calls the school principal and reports Fred.

The principal doesn't want Max to feel afraid at school. He is going to talk to Fred and his parents. Fred is in serious trouble. Fighting is against school rules.

Check Yes or No

Yes No

___ ___ 1. Max comes home from school at 3:00.

___ ___ 2. Max's face is clean.

___ ___ 3. Max's shirt is torn.

___ ___ 4. Max is sad.

___ ___ 5. Max's mother asks, "Are you hungry?"

___ ___ 6. Max tells his mother that he feels afraid.

___ ___ 7. Max doesn't want to go to school anymore.

___ ___ 8. Max tells his mother about a little girl.

___ ___ 9. Fred is mean.

___ ___ 10. Fred always wants to be friends.

___ ___ 11. Max's mother calls the school principal.

___ ___ 12. The principal is afraid of Fred.

Lesson 9: Fighting at School   53

Underline the Word from the Story

1. Max's (foot/face) is dirty.

2. Max's (shoe/shirt) is torn.

3. Max begins to (cry/laugh).

4. Max doesn't want to go to (work/school) anymore.

5. Max's mother is (surprised/afraid).

6. Fred (hits/hugs) and kicks people.

7. Fred always wants to (fight/eat).

8. Max's mother says that fighting is (good/bad).

9. Max's mother calls the school (president/principal).

10. The principal is going to talk to Fred's (uncle/parents).

Matching

Match the sentences that mean the same.

____ 1. What's wrong?   a. He is scared.

____ 2. She gives him a hug.   b. He is not nice.

____ 3. He feels afraid.   c. He is going to be punished.

____ 4. He is mean.   d. You can't do that.

____ 5. It's against the rules.   e. She puts her arms around him.

____ 6. He is in trouble.   f. What's the matter?

54   Lesson 9: Fighting at School

What Happened First?

Remember the story. Then put these events in order.

____ Max tells his mother about a big boy at school.

____ Max's mother gives him a hug.

____ The principal is going to talk to Fred and his parents.

____ Max begins to cry.

_1_ Max comes home from school.

____ Max's mother asks, "What's wrong?"

____ Max's mother calls the school principal.

Reporting a Problem

Practice the dialog with a partner.

Hello? Is this Principal Randall?

Yes. How may I help you?

I'm calling to report a problem at school.

What kind of problem?

A boy at school always fights with my son.

That is a serious problem.

Yes. My son is hurt and very upset.

Thanks for calling. Now I need more information.

Lesson 9: Fighting at School

School Rules

Read these rules from the school handbook.

The following things are not allowed at school:

1. Fighting
2. Pushing and shoving
3. Disruptive behavior
4. Bringing knives or other weapons
5. Throwing food
6. Talking back to staff
7. Disrespecting any student, staff member, or school visitor

Remember the rules. Then check Yes or No.

Yes   No

___   ___   1. Students are allowed to bring food.

___   ___   2. Students are allowed to bring weapons.

___   ___   3. Students are allowed to talk to staff.

___   ___   4. Students are allowed to disrespect visitors.

___   ___   5. Students are allowed to push and shove.

Check the Actions

Fred is in trouble for fighting. Put a check next to the things that Fred needs to do. Write your own ideas below.

___ 1. buy Max a new shirt   ___ 4. go to another school

___ 2. go to jail   ___ 5. eat lunch alone

___ 3. apologize to Max   ___ 6. stay after school

_____   _____

Problem Solving

A mean boy or girl wants to fight with your child at school. Your child is very upset. Put a check next to the good ideas. Write other good ideas on the lines below.

    ____ 1. I can tell my child to ignore the person.

    ____ 2. I can tell my child to run away from the person.

    ____ 3. I can tell my child to hit and kick the person.

    ____ 4. I can tell my child to pretend that it doesn't hurt.

    ____ 5. I can tell my child to scream for help.

    ____ 6. I can tell my child to tell the teacher or principal.

    ____ 7. I can tell my child to stop acting like a baby.

    ✓ 8. I can _____.

    ✓ 9. I can _____.

Discuss with a Partner

1. How do you know when your child is upset? Describe how your child looks and acts.

2. Do you think fighting at school is a serious problem?

3. What other problems can children have at school? Would you report these problems to the school principal? Why or why not?

Lesson 9: Fighting at School

Lesson 10

1. Does your child have homework every day?
2. Do you need to remind your child to do homework?

Too Tired for Homework

Iris is relaxing after school today. She is watching TV. She is playing with toys. She doesn't want to do her homework. She can do it later.

After dinner, Iris returns to her toys. She changes her doll's clothes. She plays with her yo-yo. Her mother says, "Do your homework!"

"OK," says Iris. But she doesn't do it. Iris walks into the bathroom. She looks in the mirror. She sticks out her tongue. She puts her fingers in her ears. She makes very funny faces.

Iris's mother is angry now. She says, "You are wasting time. You need to go to bed soon. Get busy!"

"I'm too tired," says Iris. "I can do my homework in the morning."

"I don't think so," says her mother. "You don't have time. And tomorrow, homework comes before you watch TV, play with toys, or make funny faces."

Check Yes or No

Yes   No

___ ___   1. Iris is relaxing after school.

___ ___   2. Iris is listening to the radio.

___ ___   3. Iris is playing with toys.

___ ___   4. Iris wants to do her homework.

___ ___   5. Iris returns to her toys after dinner.

___ ___   6. Iris's mother says, "Do your homework!"

___ ___   7. Iris walks into the living room.

___ ___   8. Iris looks in the mirror.

___ ___   9. Iris makes funny faces.

___ ___   10. Iris's mother is happy.

___ ___   11. Iris wants to do her homework in the morning.

___ ___   12. Iris's mother says, "That's OK."

Complete the Sentences

homework	morning	relaxing	toys
mirror	mother	tomorrow	wasting

1. The boy isn't studying. He is _____.

2. He is playing with dinosaurs and other _____.

3. His mother says, "Do your _____."

4. He has dinner with his _____ and father.

5. After dinner he makes funny faces in the _____.

6. His mother is angry. She says, "Stop _____ time."

7. The boy asks, "Can I do my homework _____?"

8. His mother answers, "You don't have time in the _____."

Matching

Match the sentences that mean the same.

____ 1. She is relaxing.   a. You are fooling around.

____ 2. Her mother is angry.   b. Do your work now.

____ 3. You are wasting time.   c. I don't have the energy.

____ 4. I'm too tired.   d. That's not OK.

____ 5. I don't think so.   e. She is taking it easy.

____ 6. Get busy.   f. Her mother is mad.

Check the Activities

Put a check next to the things your child likes to do instead of homework. Write other activities your child enjoys below.

____ watch TV

____ play with toy

____ read

____ talk on the phone

____ play outside

____ relax

____ play with friends

____ listen to music

____ play a sport

____ play video games

____ ride a bicycle

____ make funny faces

_____

_____

Homework Comes First

Practice the dialog with a partner.

Can I watch TV after dinner tonight?

No, sorry. It's time to do your homework.

But it's my favorite show!

You know the rule. Homework comes first.

Can I watch for just a few minutes?

You can watch TV when your homework is done. Get busy!

Lesson 10: Too Tired for Homework

This Week's Homework

Read the weekly homework schedule.

Homework Schedule	Monday	*Spelling:* lesson 8, pp. 32-36
Make sure your child reads at least 20 minutes a day.	Tuesday	*Math:* worksheets 53, 54, and 55
	Wednesday	*Language:* Spider Story, questions 1-7
	Thursday	*Handwriting:* lesson 11, pp. 28 and 29

My child has completed his or her homework neatly and accurately.

_____

Remember the schedule. Then complete each sentence.

1. There is handwriting homework on _____.

   Monday   Thursday

2. Your child must read at least _____ a day.

   30 minutes   20 minutes

3. The spelling lesson is on pages _____.

   32 to 36   42 to 46

4. There are _____ math work sheets.

   three   two

5. There is no homework on _____.

   Thursday   Friday

Answer the Questions

1. Does your child usually have homework?
2. Does your child have a weekly homework schedule?
3. Does your child always complete his or her homework?
4. Do you think that your child has too much homework?
5. What time of day does your child usually do homework?
6. Do you ever get angry with your child about homework?
7. Does your child have time to do homework in the morning?
8. Do you need to sign your child's homework?
9. Does your child sometimes feel too tired to do homework?

Discuss with a Partner

1. Does your child sometimes need your help with homework? What do you do when your child has an assignment that is difficult for you?
2. Do you think it's important for children to take breaks after school? Why or why not?
3. Do you think it is a parent's job to make sure that a child completes homework? Why or why not?

Lesson 11

1. Why is listening an important skill in school?
2. Does your child have spelling tests every week?

Listen and Follow Directions

Today the students are having a spelling test. Mrs. Cordua is passing out papers. She tells the children to listen and follow directions. The students need to write their names and the date on their papers. Then she tells the students to number their papers from one to ten.

Most of the students write their names, the date, and the numbers on their papers. But Tim doesn't do anything. He isn't listening. He is thinking about recess time. He wants to play ball at recess.

Mrs. Cordua begins the test. "Number one," she says. "The word is *listen*. You need to listen in class."

"Wait," says Tim. "What are we doing? I am not ready! Is this a spelling test? How many words do we have? What is the first word?"

"Sorry, Tim," says Mrs. Cordua. "Next time listen and follow directions."

Check Yes or No

Yes No

___ ___   **1.** The students are having a math test.

___ ___   **2.** Tim is passing out papers.

___ ___   **3.** Mrs. Cordua says to listen and follow directions.

___ ___   **4.** The students write their names and telephone numbers on their papers.

___ ___   **5.** The students number their papers from one to ten.

___ ___   **6.** Tim is listening.

___ ___   **7.** Tim is thinking about recess time.

___ ___   **8.** Tim wants to play on the swings at recess.

___ ___   **9.** Mrs. Cordua begins the test.

___ ___   **10.** The first word is *follow*.

___ ___   **11.** Tim is ready.

___ ___   **12.** Tim doesn't know how many words are on the test.

Underline the Word from the Story

1. The students are having a spelling (review/test).

2. Mrs. Cordua is passing out (papers/pencils).

3. The students number their papers from one to (ten/twenty).

4. Tim doesn't (play/do) anything.

5. Tim wants to play ball at (recess/lunch).

6. Tim says, "I am not (writing/ready)."

7. Mrs. Cordua says, "(Hurry/Sorry), Tim."

Unscramble the Sentences

Write the sentence on the line.

1. students   a   test.   The   having   are   spelling
   _____

2. out   is   papers.   teacher   The   passing
   _____

3. to   You   class.   listen   in   need
   _____

4. papers   Number   ten.   one   from   your   to
   _____

Who Says That?

Tim or Mrs. Cordua

1. "Listen and follow directions." _____

2. "What are we doing?" _____

3. "What is the first word?" _____

4. "Write your name and the date." _____

5. "I am not ready!" _____

6. "The word is *listen*." _____

Spelling Practice at Home

Practice the dialog with a partner.

How do you spell *follow*?

That's easy. It's f-o-l-l-o-w.

That's correct. How about *listen*?

I'm not sure. Is it l-i-s-t-e-n?

Very good! Are you ready for the spelling test tomorrow?

Yes, I am ready.

Tim's Spelling Test

Look at the teacher's comments on Tim's test.

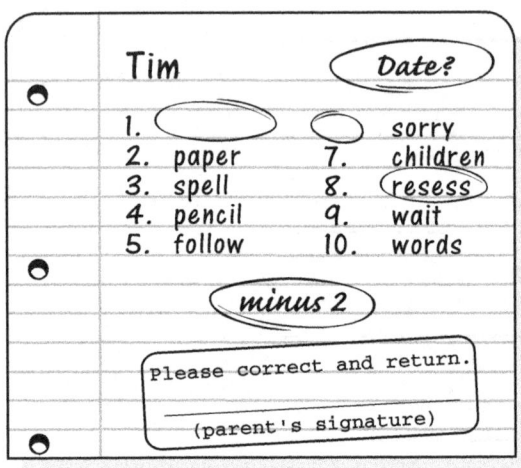

Remember Tim's test. Then complete each sentence.

1. There is no _____ on Tim's paper.

    name   date

2. Tim doesn't write a word for number _____.

    one   eight

3. The teacher marks _____ wrong on Tim's paper.

    two   three

4. The word _____ is spelled incorrectly.

    listen   recess

5. Tim needs to correct and _____ this spelling test.

    return   throw away

Problem Solving

Your child is not listening in class. The teacher says that your child is not following directions. Put a check next to the good ideas. Write other good ideas on the lines below.

____ 1. I can talk to my child about listening better.

____ 2. I can take my child to the doctor for a hearing test.

____ 3. I can get angry and yell at my child.

____ 4. I can reward my child when he or she listens well.

____ 5. I can put my child in a different class.

____ 6. I can take my child to a counselor.

____ 7. I can tell the teacher that he or she is boring.

✓ 8. I can _____.

✓ 9. I can _____.

Discuss with a Partner

1. What does Tim learn from his experience with the spelling test? Do you think the teacher does the right thing? Why or why not?

2. How do you help your child prepare for tests?

Lesson 12

1. Do you have rules about bedtime?
2. What time does your child go to bed on school nights?

It's Bedtime

Mary is six years old. Her bedtime is 8:00. Mary needs 10 hours of sleep a night. She has to get up early for school.

At 7:45 Mary's mother tells her that it is almost bedtime. Mary needs to put on her pajamas and brush her teeth. "You need to be in bed in fifteen minutes," says Mary's mother.

Mary doesn't want to go to bed. She isn't sleepy. Mary wants to stay up until 9:00 like her older sister. "Can I please stay up a little later?" asks Mary.

"No," answers Mary's mother. "Your bedtime is eight o'clock. That's the rule. You are very young. Your body needs rest. I don't want you to feel tired at school tomorrow."

Mary is sad. Mary's mother says, "Tomorrow is Friday. You can stay up a little later tomorrow night. You don't have school on Saturday."

Mary smiles. She is happy now. Bedtime will be later on Friday!

Check Yes or No

Yes   No

____ ____ 1. Mary is six years old.

____ ____ 2. Mary's bedtime is 8:30.

____ ____ 3. Mary needs 12 hours of sleep a night.

____ ____ 4. Mary needs to get up early for school.

____ ____ 5. Mary needs to put on her pajamas.

____ ____ 6. Mary wants to go to bed.

____ ____ 7. Mary isn't sleepy.

____ ____ 8. Mary's sister goes to bed at 8:00.

____ ____ 9. Mary's mother lets her stay up a little later.

____ ____ 10. There is a rule about bedtime.

____ ____ 11. Mary has school on Saturday.

____ ____ 12. Bedtime is 8:00 on Friday.

Complete the Story

| bedtime | later | pajamas | rule |
| hours | older | rest | sleepy |

Joseph is 11 years old. His _____ is 9:00. Joseph
                                    1
needs 10 _____ of sleep a night.
           2

At 8:50 Joseph's father tells him that it's almost bedtime. Joseph

needs to put on his _____. Joseph's father says, "You
                           3
need to be in bed in ten minutes."

Joseph doesn't want to go to bed. He isn't _____.
                                                   4
He wants to stay up until 10:00 like his _____ brother.
                                                 5
"Can I please stay up a little later?" asks Joseph.

"No," answers Joseph's father. "Your bedtime is nine o'clock.

That's the _____. Your body needs _____."
                6   7

Joseph is upset. His father says, "Joseph, tomorrow is Friday.

Then you can stay up _____."
                            8

Joseph smiles. Friday is the best day of the week.

72   Lesson 12: It's Bedtime

Check the Rules

Put a check next to an item if your family has rules about it. Write other items that need rules below.

___ bedtime   ___ television   ___ strangers

___ friends   ___ computer   ___ money

___ schoolwork   ___ arguing   ___ telephone

___ food   ___ housework   ___ clothes

_____   _____   _____   _____

Time for Bed

Practice the dialog with a partner.

It's a quarter to nine. It's almost bedtime.

Can I stay up until nine thirty?

No, you need rest.

I'm too old to have a bedtime.

Sorry. Nine o'clock is the rule on a school night.

I can't wait until the weekend.

Does Your Child Need More Sleep?

Read the brochure from the doctor's office.

Your school-age child needs 10 to 12 hours of sleep each night.

Sleep helps children:
- grow tall and strong
- be healthy
- stay alert
- get good grades
- be happy

Remember the brochure. Then complete each sentence.

1. This brochure is from the _____ office.

   school   doctor's

2. This information is about a _____ child.

   preschool-age   school-age

3. A child needs _____ of sleep a night.

   between 10 and 12 hours   between 10 and 11 hours

4. Sleep helps children grow _____.

   tall and strong   short and weak

5. Sleep helps children stay _____.

   alert   alarmed

Lesson 12: It's Bedtime

Answer the Questions

1. How old is your child?
2. Does your child have a bedtime?
3. How many hours of sleep does your child get each night?
4. Do you need to tell your child when it's bedtime?
5. What does your child do before going to bed?
6. Does your child want to go to bed?
7. Do you sometimes allow your child to stay up late?
8. Is your child tired in the morning?
9. What other rules does your family have?
10. Do you need to remind your child about following rules?

Discuss with a Partner

1. Can a child who isn't sleeping enough do well in school? How does a sleepy child act in school?
2. Do you think older children and younger children need the same amount of sleep? Why or why not?
3. What can you do to help your child fall asleep?

Lesson 13

1. Where do you take your child shopping for shoes?
2. How much money do you usually spend on shoes?

Expensive Shoes

Tamika and her son Jamal are at the shopping center. Jamal needs new shoes. Tamika and Jamal go into the shoe store. There are a lot of shoes inside. Jamal walks around the store. Tamika looks at the price tags on the shoes.

Jamal points to some shoes on a table. "I want those shoes," says Jamal. "Everyone wears them at school."

Tamika looks at the price tag. They are $100! They are very expensive. Tamika shakes her head. She doesn't want to pay $100. "Please, Mom!" says Jamal. "I really want them!"

Tamika shows Jamal some other shoes. They are on

sale. They are a little different, but they are good shoes. And they are much cheaper. They are only $30. Tamika wants to buy the $30 shoes.

Tamika tells Jamal that $100 is too much to spend on shoes. His feet are growing. The shoes will be too small soon. Then they will have to buy new shoes again.

Jamal is sad and angry. He doesn't want the $30 shoes. He doesn't want to look at them. Jamal wants the shoes that everyone wears.

Check Yes or No

Yes   No

____ ____ 1. Tamika and Jamal are at home.

____ ____ 2. Jamal needs a new jacket.

____ ____ 3. Tamika and Jamal go into the shoe store.

____ ____ 4. Tamika looks at the price tags on the shoes.

____ ____ 5. Jamal wants shoes that cost $30.

____ ____ 6. Tamika shows Jamal some other shoes.

____ ____ 7. The other shoes are on sale.

____ ____ 8. The $30 shoes look just like the $100 shoes.

____ ____ 9. The shoes on sale are $50.

____ ____ 10. Jamal's feet are growing.

What Is the Category?

angry	clothing store	sandals	sneakers
bookstore	disappointed	shoe store	surprised
boots	sad	shoes	toy store

Shops

1. _____
2. _____
3. _____
4. _____

Emotions

1. _____
2. _____
3. _____
4. _____

Footwear

1. _____
2. _____
3. _____
4. _____

Same Meaning

Copy the word or phrase from the story that has the same meaning as the phrase below.

1. feet are getting bigger _____

2. moves her head from side to side _____

3. not exactly the same _____

4. much less expensive _____

5. cost a lot of money _____

6. unhappy and mad _____

Who Says That?

Tamika or Jamal

1. "I don't like these cheap shoes." _____

2. "I want the shoes my friends have." _____

3. "Sorry, these shoes are too expensive." _____

4. "Your feet are still growing." _____

5. "Please, Mom!" _____

An Argument in the Shoe Store

Practice the dialog with a partner.

I want those shoes.

Let me look at the price tag. Oh, they're too expensive!

But everyone wears them at school!

How about these shoes? They're only $30.

Those aren't in style. Nobody wears those shoes.

You can be the first one!

Lesson 13: Expensive Shoes

Come to Shoe Palace!

Listen to the radio ad.

> Shoe Palace has the shoes you want! We carry all the name brands, and we have hundreds of styles to choose from. Come and see our wide selection of sale shoes marked from 30 to 60% off. We are located on North Shore Boulevard in the Fashion Square Shopping Center. Parking is free. Our hours are Monday through Friday from 9:00 to 7:00, Saturday from 10:00 to 7:00, and Sunday from 11:00 to 6:00. See you there!

Remember the ad. Then complete each sentence.

1. Shoe Palace is open on _____ from 10:00 to 7:00.

    Saturday   Sunday

2. Shoe Palace is in the Fashion _____ Shopping Center.

    Square   Plaza

3. The sale shoes are marked _____ off.

    from 30 to 50%   from 30 to 60%

4. Parking _____.

    costs $5   is free

5. The hours are _____ Monday through Friday.

    9:00 to 7:00   10:00 to 8:00

Lesson 13: Expensive Shoes

Problem Solving

Your child wants an expensive pair of shoes. He or she doesn't want to look at a cheaper pair. Put a check next to the good ideas. Write other ideas on the lines below.

____ 1. I can buy the expensive shoes and make my child happy.

____ 2. I can get angry and leave the store.

____ 3. I can offer to pay for half of the shoes.

____ 4. I can ask a clerk when the shoes will go on sale.

____ 5. I can explain to my child that I can't afford them.

____ 6. I can convince my child that the cheaper shoes look nice.

____ 7. I can ask other parents at school to buy cheaper shoes.

✔ 8. I can _____.

✔ 9. I can _____.

Discuss with a Partner

1. How often do you need to buy shoes for your child? What types of shoes does your child have?

2. How do you help your child make good choices when shopping for clothes and shoes? What do you say if your child wants something because another child has it?

Lesson 13: Expensive Shoes

Lesson 14

1. How does your child get to school?
2. Is there a lot of traffic in your area?

Crossing the Street

Natalie walks to school. She needs to cross many streets between her apartment and the school. Natalie waits at every corner. She looks to the left and to the right. When there are no cars or buses, she crosses the street.

Some corners have traffic lights. There are "Walk" and "Don't Walk" signs. Natalie doesn't cross until she sees a "Walk" sign.

Natalie's school is on a busy street. There is a crosswalk in front of the school. Two white lines are painted on the street. Students walk between the white lines from one side of the street to the other.

In the morning, a crossing guard stands on the corner. She blows a whistle and stops the traffic. She tells the children when it's safe to cross.

Natalie is very careful crossing streets. She doesn't want to get hurt. She wants to get to school safely.

Check Yes or No

Yes No

____ ____ 1. Natalie walks to school.

____ ____ 2. Natalie doesn't need to cross any streets.

____ ____ 3. Natalie runs at every corner.

____ ____ 4. Natalie looks to the left and to the right.

____ ____ 5. When Natalie sees a bus, she crosses the street.

____ ____ 6. Every corner has a traffic light.

____ ____ 7. There are "Walk" and "Don't Walk" signs.

____ ____ 8. Natalie's school is on a quiet street.

____ ____ 9. There is a bus stop in front of the school.

____ ____ 10. Two green lines are painted on the street.

____ ____ 11. A crossing guard is on the corner in the morning.

____ ____ 12. Natalie is very careful crossing streets.

Complete the Sentences

apartment	crosswalk	streets	whistle
careful	left	traffic	white

1. Maddy lives in an _____.

2. She crosses many _____ on her way to school.

3. Maddy looks to the _____ and to the right.

4. Some corners have _____ lights.

5. There is a _____ in front of the school.

6. Maddy walks between the _____ lines.

7. The crossing guard blows a _____.

8. Maddy is _____ crossing streets.

Matching

Match the sentences that mean the same.

____ 1. She is very careful.   a. You can go to the other side of the street.

____ 2. Look left and right.   b. Cars stop moving for him.

____ 3. It's a busy street.   c. Look both ways.

____ 4. He stops the traffic.   d. She watches out.

____ 5. It's safe to cross.   e. There is a lot of traffic.

84   Lesson 14: Crossing the Street

Who Says That?

Crossing Guard or Natalie

1. "Watch out!" _____

2. "I look both ways before I cross the street." _____

3. "Are there any cars coming?" _____

4. "It is safe for you to cross now." _____

5. "I am walking to school." _____

Conversation at the Corner

Practice the dialog with a partner.

You can't cross yet.

There are no cars coming.

You need to wait until I blow the whistle and stop traffic.

Why is that?

A car could turn the corner and hit you.

You're right. Thanks for the warning.

Crossing the Street

Circle the picture of each child who is being careful.
What is each child doing?

1.   2.    3.    4.

1. _____

2. _____

3. _____

4. _____

Make a List

List safe ways for a child to get to school.

1. _____   3. _____

2. _____   4. _____

List dangerous ways for a child to get to school.

1. _____   3. _____

2. _____   4. _____

Answer the Questions

1. Does your child walk to school?
2. Does your child sometimes cross streets alone?
3. Is your child usually careful crossing streets?
4. Is there a crosswalk in front of your child's school?
5. Is there a crossing guard or safety patrol?
6. Is there an adult in front of the school directing traffic?
7. What is the speed limit in front of the school?
8. Do you always obey traffic lights when you are walking?
9. Do you ever cross a street when there is a "Don't Walk" sign?

Discuss with a Partner

1. What do you say to your child about traffic safety? Why is talking about it important?
2. Do people obey traffic laws in your city? Are the streets safe for people who walk or ride bicycles?
3. What do green, red, and yellow traffic lights mean? What traffic signs do you see? What do they mean?

Lesson 15

1. Is your child sometimes absent from school? Why?
2. Do you always call and report your child's absence?

Absent from School

Willie doesn't feel well this morning. He has a fever. Willie can't go to school. He needs to rest at home.

Willie's father calls the office at school. He tells the attendance clerk that his son is absent today. He says that Willie is sick.

"What is your son's full name?" asks the clerk. Then she asks, "What grade is he in? And who is his teacher? Also, do you know his room number?" Willie's father answers all her questions. Then the clerk thanks him for calling.

Willie's father stays home from work. He calls his work and explains that he needs to take care of his son.

Willie rests at home all day. His father gives him some medicine for his fever.

In the evening, Willie feels a little better, but he still has a fever. He can't go to school tomorrow. He needs to rest one more day. Tomorrow Willie's mother needs to stay home from work and take care of him. She will call the office at school in the morning.

Check Yes or No

Yes   No

___ ___   1. Willie feels well this morning.

___ ___   2. Willie has a fever.

___ ___   3. Willie can go to school.

___ ___   4. Willie's father calls the doctor.

___ ___   5. The attendance clerk asks for Willie's grade.

___ ___   6. Willie's father goes to work.

___ ___   7. Willie rests at home all day.

___ ___   8. Willie takes medicine for his fever.

___ ___   9. In the evening, Willie feels worse.

___ ___   10. Willie can go to school tomorrow.

___ ___   11. Willie's mother needs to stay home from work tomorrow.

What Is the Category?

attendance clerk	father	mother	son
daughter	fever	principal	sore throat
earache	math teacher	school nurse	stomachache

Health Problems

1. _____
2. _____
3. _____
4. _____

Family Members

1. _____
2. _____
3. _____
4. _____

People at School

1. _____
2. _____
3. _____
4. _____

Matching

Match the parts of the sentences.

___ 1. He doesn't feel   a. his room number?

___ 2. Do you know   b. the office at school.

___ 3. What grade is   c. for calling.

___ 4. He can't go   d. him medicine for his fever.

___ 5. His father calls   e. to school tomorrow.

___ 6. His father gives   f. he in?

___ 7. The clerk thanks him   g. well this morning.

What Happened First?

Remember the story. Then put these events in order.

____ The clerk thanks Willie's father for calling.

____ Willie's father calls his work.

_1_ Willie has a fever.

____ The clerk asks for his son's full name.

____ Willie's mother will call the office at school.

____ Willie feels a little better.

____ Willie's father calls the office at school.

My Son Is Sick

Practice the dialog with a partner.

I'm calling to report my son's absence.

Is he ill?

Yes, he has a fever and a sore throat.

What are your son's name and grade?

His name is Willie Shea. He is in the third grade.

Thanks for calling. I hope Willie feels better soon.

Thank you.

A Message from the School

Listen to the message from the school office.

> Good morning. This is Ellen James from the attendance office at Emerson Elementary School. Your daughter Gwen isn't at school today. We need you to call the office and explain her absence. Today is Wednesday, September 30, and it's now 10:30 A.M. The phone number is 555-3341. Thank you.

Remember the message. Then complete each sentence.

1. The clerk's first name is _____.

    Helen   Ellen

2. The clerk is calling from the _____.

    classroom   office

3. The name of the school is _____ Elementary.

    Emerson   Edison

4. Today's date is _____.

    September 13   September 30

5. The telephone number is _____.

    555-3341   555-3411

Problem Solving

Your child is sick, and you can't stay home from work to take care of him or her. Put a check next to the good ideas. Write other ideas on the lines below.

____ 1. I can ask a relative to take care of him or her.

____ 2. I can bring my sick child to work with me.

____ 3. I can ask a neighbor to watch my child.

____ 4. I can quit my job if I can't stay home.

____ 5. I can send my sick child to school.

____ 6. I can have my child rest in the school nurse's office.

____ 7. I can leave my child home alone.

✔ 8. I can _____.

✔ 9. I can _____.

Discuss with a Partner

1. What are some important reasons for children to stay home from school? What are unimportant reasons?

2. What are some common childhood illnesses? What are some ways to treat them?

3. Why do you sometimes need to bring your child to a doctor?

Answer Key

Lesson 1

Check Yes or No (p. 5)

1. yes
2. no
3. no
4. no
5. no
6. yes
7. yes
8. no
9. yes
10. yes
11. yes
12. no

Complete the Story (p. 6)

1. school
2. bus
3. tired
4. clock
5. minutes
6. teeth
7. corner
8. driver

What Happened First? (p. 7)

3, 5, 7, 4, 1, 6, 2

A Message from the Principal (p. 8)

1. Ancheta
2. Foster
3. Marc
4. at the office
5. 555-8794

Lesson 2

Check Yes or No (p. 11)

1. no
2. yes
3. yes
4. no
5. no
6. yes
7. no
8. yes
9. no
10. yes
11. yes
12. yes

Complete the Sentences (p. 12)

1. cover
2. below
3. headache
4. lines
5. office
6. chart
7. copy
8. parents

Matching (p. 12)

1. c
2. d
3. a
4. e
5. b

What Happened First? (p. 13)

5, 6, 4, 7, 1, 3, 2

Family Eye Care (p. 14)

1. Luskin
2. adults and children
3. from 9:00 to 5:00
4. 1018 Grape Street
5. 555-6813

Lesson 3

Check Yes or No (p. 17)

1. yes
2. no
3. no
4. no
5. yes
6. no
7. yes
8. no
9. no
10. yes
11. yes
12. yes

Complete the Story (p. 18)

1. years
2. only
3. Welcome
4. shy
5. empty
6. chair
7. Japanese
8. friends

Personal Information Form (p. 20)

Last Name: Cruz
First Name: Carmen
Age: 7
Native Country: Mexico
Native Language: Spanish

Lesson 4

Check Yes or No (p. 23)

1. yes
2. no
3. no
4. no
5. yes
6. yes
7. yes
8. yes
9. no
10. no
11. yes

Underline the Word from the Story (p. 24)

1. morning
2. kitchen
3. hungry
4. student
5. cafeteria
6. every day

Unscramble the Sentences (p. 24)

1. Lamar is getting ready for school.
2. Do you have time for a bowl of cereal?
3. There is a breakfast program at school.
4. A good breakfast helps him pay attention.

This Week's Breakfast Menu (p. 26)

1. Tuesday
2. Monday and Friday
3. Tuesday or Thursday
4. every day
5. peaches

Lesson 5

Check Yes or No (p. 29)

1. no
2. no
3. yes
4. yes
5. no
6. yes
7. no
8. no
9. yes
10. yes
11. yes

What Is the Category? (p. 30)

People	Emotions	School Subjects
1. librarian	1. concerned	1. arithmetic
2. parent	2. happy	2. reading
3. student	3. proud	3. spelling
4. teacher	4. worried	4. writing

Same Meaning (p. 30)

1. very smart
2. smile
3. It's difficult for him.
4. behind the other students
5. parent and teacher conference

Library Information (p. 32)

1. Mission Park
2. 11th and 12th
3. Monday and Wednesday
4. from 9:30 A.M. to 5:30 P.M.
5. open

Lesson 6

Check Yes or No (p. 35)
1. no
2. yes
3. no
4. yes
5. no
6. no
7. no
8. yes
9. yes
10. no
11. yes

Underline the Word from the Story (p. 36)
1. grade
2. Tuesday
3. classroom
4. between
5. hand
6. addition
7. students

Unscramble the Sentences (p. 36)
1. Lili is in the first grade.
2. Her mother volunteers in the classroom.
3. She helps them learn addition.
4. Mei corrects papers for the teacher.

Who Says That? (p. 37)
1. Mei 2. Lili 3. Lili 4. Mei 5. Lili

Who Needs Help? (p. 38)
1. raising her hand (circled)
2. reading
3. writing
4. looking confused (circled)

Lesson 7

Check Yes or No (p. 41)
1. no
2. yes
3. no
4. no
5. yes
6. yes
7. no
8. no
9. yes
10. no
11. no
12. yes

Complete the Sentences (p. 42)
1. suggests
2. ready
3. language
4. tired
5. backpack
6. note
7. important
8. tests

Matching (p. 42)
1. d 2. e 3. a 4. b 5. f 6. c

A Letter to Parents (p. 44)
1. parents
2. May 1
3. will not be
4. skills
5. nutritious

Lesson 8

Check Yes or No (p. 47)
1. yes
2. no
3. yes
4. no
5. no
6. yes
7. yes
8. yes
9. yes
10. no
11. no

Complete the Story (p. 48)
1. excited
2. sign up
3. girls
4. uniforms
5. friends
6. information
7. money
8. questions

Youth Soccer Information (p. 50)
1. 1251 Ivy
2. Saturday
3. from 9:00 to 12:00
4. uniform
5. birth certificate

Lesson 9

Check Yes or No (p. 53)
1. no
2. no
3. yes
4. yes
5. no
6. yes
7. yes
8. no
9. yes
10. no
11. yes
12. no

Underline the Word from the Story (p. 54)
1. face
2. shirt
3. cry
4. school
5. surprised
6. hits
7. fight
8. bad
9. principal
10. parents

Matching (p. 54)
1. f 2. e 3. a 4. b 5. d 6. c

What Happened First? (p. 55)
4, 5, 7, 3, 1, 2, 6

School Rules (p. 56)
1. yes 2. no 3. yes 4. no 5. no

Lesson 10

Check Yes or No (p. 59)
1. yes
2. no
3. yes
4. no
5. yes
6. yes
7. no
8. yes
9. yes
10. no
11. yes
12. no

Complete the Sentences (p. 60)
1. relaxing
2. toys
3. homework
4. mother
5. mirror
6. wasting
7. tomorrow
8. morning

Matching (p. 60)
1. e 2. f 3. a 4. c 5. d 6. b

This Week's Homework (p. 62)
1. Thursday
2. 20 minutes
3. 32 to 36
4. three
5. Friday

Lesson 11

Check Yes or No (p. 65)
1. no
2. no
3. yes
4. no
5. yes
6. no
7. yes
8. no
9. yes
10. no
11. no
12. yes

Underline the Word from the Story (p. 66)
1. test
2. papers
3. ten
4. do
5. recess
6. ready
7. Sorry

Answer Key 95

Unscramble the Sentences (p. 66)
1. The students are having a spelling test.
2. The teacher is passing out papers.
3. You need to listen in class.
4. Number your papers from one to ten.

Who Says That? (p. 67)
1. Mrs. Cordua   3. Tim   5. Tim
2. Tim   4. Mrs. Cordua 6. Mrs. Cordua

Tim's Spelling Test (p. 68)
1. date   2. one   3. two   4. recess   5. return

Lesson 12

Check Yes or No (p. 71)
1. yes   4. yes   7. yes   10. yes
2. no   5. yes   8. no   11. no
3. no   6. no   9. no   12. no

Complete the Story (p. 72)
1. bedtime   3. pajamas   5. older   7. rest
2. hours   4. sleepy   6. rule   8. later

Does Your Child Need More Sleep? (p. 74)
1. doctor's   4. tall and strong
2. school-age   5. alert
3. between 10 and 12 hours

Lesson 13

Check Yes or No (p. 77)
1. no   4. yes   7. yes   10. yes
2. no   5. no   8. no
3. yes   6. yes   9. no

What Is the Category? (p. 78)

Shops	Emotions	Footwear
1. bookstore	1. angry	1. boots
2. clothing store	2. disappointed	2. sandals
3. shoe store	3. sad	3. shoes
4. toy store	4. surprised	4. sneakers

Same Meaning (p. 78)
1. feet are growing   4. much cheaper
2. shakes her head   5. are very expensive
3. a little different   6. sad and angry

Who Says That? (p. 79)
1. Jamal   3. Tamika   5. Jamal
2. Jamal   4. Tamika

Come to Shoe Palace! (p. 80)
1. Saturday   3. from 30 to 60%   5. 9:00 to 7:00
2. Square   4. is free

Lesson 14

Check Yes or No (p. 83)
1. yes   4. yes   7. yes   10. no
2. no   5. no   8. no   11. yes
3. no   6. no   9. no   12. yes

Complete the Sentences (p. 84)
1. apartment   4. traffic   7. whistle
2. streets   5. crosswalk   8. careful
3. left   6. white

Matching (p. 84)
1. d   2. c   3. e   4. b   5. a

Who Says That? (p. 85)
1. Crossing Guard   3. Natalie   5. Natalie
2. Natalie   4. Crossing Guard

Crossing the Street (p. 86)
1. waiting to cross the street (circled)
2. walking outside the crosswalk
3. waiting for the crossing guard to say it's OK to cross the street (circled)
4. crossing in front of a car

Lesson 15

Check Yes or No (p. 89)
1. no   4. no   7. yes   10. no
2. yes   5. yes   8. yes   11. yes
3. no   6. no   9. no

What Is the Category? (p. 90)

Health Problems	Family Members	People at School
1. earache	1. daughter	1. attendance clerk
2. fever	2. father	2. math teacher
3. sore throat	3. mother	3. principal
4. stomachache	4. son	4. school nurse

Matching (p. 90)
1. g   2. a   3. f   4. e   5. b   6. d   7. c

What Happened First? (p. 91)
4, 5, 1, 3, 7, 6, 2

A Message from the School (p. 92)
1. Ellen   4. September 30
2. office   5. 555-3341
3. Emerson